Doggy Desserts

Homemade Treats for Happy, Healthy Dogs

By Cheryl Gianfrancesco

Karla Austin, *Business Operations Manager*
Nick Clemente, *Special Consultant*
Barbara Kimmel, *Managing Editor*
Jessica Knott, *Production Supervisor*
Heather Powers, *Design*
Indexed by Melody Englund

Photographs on pages 1, 4, 6, 12, 13, 15-19, 26, 29, 36, 40, 45-48, 50, 53-54, 57, 59-61, 64-65, 70-74, 77-78, 83, 86-87, 90, 93, 99, 100, 105, 107 Copyright © 2006 by Tara Gregg, Sporthorse Photography. Photographs on pages 5 and 32 Copyright © 2006 by Cheryl Gianfrancesco. Photographs on pages 14, 24, 44, 56, 63, 96 Copyright © 2006 by Diane Lewis. Photographs on pages 21-22, 25, 28, 30, 33-35, 39, 42-43, 58, 62, 66, 81-82, 84, 91-92, 95, 97, 100, 102-104, 106, 108-109 by photos.com. Food styled by Laura Hathaway.

Library of Congress Cataloging-in-Publication Data

Gianfrancesco, Cheryl, 1966–
  Doggy desserts : homemade treats for happy, healthy dogs / by Cheryl Gianfrancesco ; photographs by Tara Gregg.
    p. cm.
  Includes index.
  ISBN-13: 978-1-931993-80-7
  1. Dog—Food—Recipes. 2. Desserts. I. Title.

  SF427.4.G5294 2007
  636.7'085—dc22
  1. 2. I. Title.

BowTie Press®
A Division of BowTie, Inc.
3 Burroughs
Irvine, California 92618

Dedication

This book is dedicated to Kooper, my best friend, who taught me more about love and life than words can express—you will be forever in my heart; and to my mother, who with love and patience taught me how to bake. This book would not have been possible without you both. I miss and love you both very much.

Contents

Introduction

I will never forget the first time I saw Kooper: a ball of golden brown fur with a wet spot on his forehead from the water bottle in his cage and the sweetest brown eyes I have ever seen. I knew instantly he was the dog for me. I was so excited to finally have a dog of my own. As a young puppy, Kooper was very ill; he could not eat store-bought dog food, and he was on a very strict veterinary diet, which did not include treats. Like any new pet owner, I wanted to spoil my new puppy rotten, and to me, not being able to toss Kooper a much-earned reward was unacceptable. I searched pet stores and any dog treat recipes I could find, but most included salt, sugar, and artificial colorings. My frustration motivated me to make my own treats for Kooper. The treats had to be healthy and tasty as well as easy to make. I have often shared these treats (against Kooper's wishes) with friends who have dogs. After six years, I have decided to share my recipes that were only for Kooper and his friends. I hope your special loved one enjoys these treats, which will be homemade with your love.

Baking Notes

Allergies

Some animals may be allergic to some of the ingredients in these recipes. If your dog has not been exposed to any of the ingredients listed, I suggest that you pick a recipe that has very few ingredients. Give your dog half the treat and wait an hour. If you notice increased scratching, vomiting, diarrhea, swelling, or any strange behavior, contact your veterinarian or emergency animal facility immediately. If you observe no reaction, increase the amount of the treat you originally gave your dog. Again, wait an hour. Continue this process until you are certain there is no reaction, and use the same procedure when introducing other new ingredients to your dog.

Treats, Not Meals

These recipes make wholesome treats for your dog as they contain no artificial coloring, preservatives, flavorings, fillers, or chemicals. However, they are treats only and are not intended as a complete diet.

Ingredients

When purchasing ingredients, choose the best quality you can find and afford. Organic and non-organic ingredients are both fine, so use whatever you prefer.

Any type of flour can be used in these recipes, especially if your dog has a wheat allergy. If you use white flour, I suggest buying unbleached white flour.

When deciding what cheese to use, the choice is yours. In my recipes, I suggest low-fat cheeses. And purchase all-natural, unsalted peanut butter with no sugar added; most grocery stores carry natural peanut butter.

Salt and Sugar

Salt and sugar are not good for your dog, so look for products with no salt or sugar added.

Carob, Not Chocolate

Because chocolate can be fatal to your dog, carob is used extensively in these recipes. Carob is a chocolate substitute that is very nutritious and is available at health food stores and many grocery stores.

Eggs

Recipes that call for eggs mean egg whites and yolks, not the shells. I have seen many dog recipes that contain eggshells. Eggshells can have chemicals, bacteria, and a host of other items that can make your dog very sick.

Mixing

Cakes and muffins can be mixed with a fork. Cookies and frostings should be mixed with either a hand or stand-alone mixer. When mixing, if your dough does not seem firm enough, add more flour, one tablespoon at a time. Mix or knead in the flour until the dough is firm. If your dough is too stiff and crumbly, add more water, one tablespoon at a time.

Yield

The yields for the recipes provided are just guidelines; your yield may be more or less depending on the cookie cutter you use and the thickness of your dough. Be creative when baking, and use cookie cutters with a variety of shapes.

Oven Temperature

Variations in oven temperatures are common. Your oven temperature and the thickness of your dough may cause your desserts to bake quicker or take longer than expected. Check all items periodically during baking. All temperatures listed refer to degrees Fahrenheit. If your dog does not like hard, crunchy treats, eliminate the suggested oven drying time of one to two hours. The drying time removes the moisture from the cookie, making them hard. If you do not dry the cookies after baking, they will be chewy instead of crunchy.

Storage

These recipes do not have any preservatives to extend their life, so store them accordingly. I normally store treats in an airtight plastic container in a cool dry place, although I do refrigerate cakes, muffins, and treats that contain meat or cheese. The estimated average shelf life of most of the treats is approximately three weeks for cookies and one and one-half to two weeks for cakes and muffins. The longevity of the treats depends on the freshness of ingredients used and the climate in which the treats are stored. As a final note, be sure to cool all food items completely before serving them to your dog.

Grapes, Raisins, and Garlic Warning

Since the development of this book, there has been evidence that grapes, raisins, and garlic can be toxic to some dogs. To be safe, we recommend that you omit these ingredients from the recipes in this book. Omitting them will not alter the palatability or consistency of the treat.

Cookies

Carob Balls

Ingredients

½ cup all natural apple-sauce, no sugar added

⅓ cup honey

1 Tbsp vegetable oil

1 tsp pure vanilla extract

2 cups whole wheat flour

¼ cup carob powder❧

2 tsp baking soda

In a large bowl, mix all the ingredients. With your hands, make small balls with the dough, about an inch in diameter. You may vary the size depending on the size of your dog, but be careful not to make the carob balls too big; your dog may have difficulty swallowing them. Place the balls 1½ inches apart on a baking sheet. Bake at 350 degrees for 15 to 17 minutes. When done, the cookies should be firm to the touch. Turn the oven off, and leave the cookies in for 1 to 2 hours to harden.

Yield: Approximately 65 one-inch carob balls

❧Available at health food stores and some grocery stores

Carob Peanut Butter Crunch Balls

½ cup all natural peanut butter, no salt or sugar added
¼ cup honey

1 cup puffed rice cereal, not
   sugared
1 cup carob chips 🐾

In a large bowl, beat the peanut butter and honey until well blended and smooth. Stir in the cereal, and mix well. Use a teaspoon to shape the mixture into balls. Place the balls on a baking sheet lined with wax paper. Chill until firm. When the mixture is firm, melt the carob chips in a double boiler over low heat, stirring until melted. Pierce the balls with a fork, and dip them into the carob, completely coating each ball. Shake off the excess carob, and return the ball to the baking sheet. Place the baking sheet in refrigerator for 1 hour or until the carob is completely hardened. Store the crunch balls in a covered container or plastic storage bag in the refrigerator.

Yield: Approximately 20 two-inch balls
🐾 Available at health food stores and some grocery stores

Salmon Balls

Ingredients

4 oz canned salmon, drained, rinsed, and bones removed

$^1/_2$ Tbsp dried parsley or 1 Tbsp fresh parsley

1 $^2/_3$ cups unbleached white flour

$^1/_2$ Tbsp garlic powder

2 Tbsp water

1 egg

In a large bowl, mix all the ingredients. Knead the dough on a lightly floured surface until firm. Roll out the dough to $^1/_4$-inch thickness, and cut out shapes with a cookie cutter. Put the cookies on a baking sheet, $^1/_2$ inch apart. Bake at 375 degrees for 30 to 35 minutes. When done, the cookies should be firm to the touch. Turn the oven off, and leave the cookies in the oven for 1 to 2 hours to harden.

Yield: Approximately 33 two-inch cookies

Ginger Carob Biscotti

Ingredients

2 ½ cups whole wheat flour

2 tsp carob powderd

2 Tbsp ground ginger

1 egg

¼ cup honey

1 tsp pure vanilla extract

½ cup water

In a large bowl, mix all the ingredients. Knead the dough on a lightly floured surface until firm. Separate the dough into two equal portions. On a baking sheet, roll one portion with a rolling pin to form a rectangle approximately 4½ to 5 inches by 11 to 12 inches. Repeat with the other half of the dough. Depending on the size of your baking sheet, both pieces of rolled-out dough should fit on the same baking sheet. Bake at 375 degrees for 30 to 35 minutes. Cookies are done when a toothpick inserted in the center comes out clean. Remove the cookies and cut them into 1- by 3-inch slices. Return the cut cookie slices to the oven, and bake them again at 375 degrees for 10 minutes. Remove the biscotti, turn them over, and bake them for an additional 10 minutes. Turn the oven off, and let the biscotti sit in the oven 1 to 2 hours to harden.

Yield: Approximately 50 biscotti

❖Available at health food stores and some grocery stores

Almond Biscotti

¼ cup almonds, finely chopped

3 ½ cups whole wheat flour

½ tsp baking powder

½ tsp baking soda

½ tsp ground cinnamon

2 Tbsp vegetable oil

½ cup honey

3 egg whites

1 egg

1 tsp pure vanilla extract

1 tsp orange rind, grated

¼ cup water

In a large bowl, mix all the ingredients. Knead the dough on a lightly floured surface until firm. Separate the dough into two equal portions. Roll out the dough with a rolling pin to form a rectangle on a baking sheet, about 4½ to 5 inches by 11 to 12 inches. Repeat with the other half of the dough. Depending on the size of your baking sheet, both pieces of rolled-out dough should fit on the same baking sheet. Bake at 375 degrees for 30 to 35 minutes. Cookies are done when a toothpick inserted and removed from the center comes out clean. Remove and cut into 1- by 3-inch slices. Return the cut cookie slices to the oven, and bake at 375 degrees for 10 minutes. Remove the biscotti from the oven, turn them over, and bake an additional 10 minutes. Turn the oven off, and leave the biscotti in for 1 to 2 hours to harden.

Yield: Approximately 65 biscotti

Walnut Biscotti

Ingredients

2 cups whole wheat
    flour
$\frac{1}{4}$ cup honey
1 tsp baking powder
$\frac{1}{4}$ cup vegetable oil

$\frac{1}{4}$ cup water
1 egg
$\frac{1}{2}$ cup unsalted walnuts,
    chopped

In a large bowl, mix all the ingredients. Knead the dough on a lightly floured surface until firm. Separate the dough into two equal portions. Roll out the dough with a rolling pin to form a rectangle on a baking sheet, about $4\frac{1}{2}$ to 5 inches by 11 to 12 inches. Repeat with the other half of the dough. Depending on the size of your baking sheet, both pieces of rolled-out dough should fit on the same baking sheet. Bake at 375 degrees for 30 to 35 minutes. Cookies are done when a toothpick inserted in the center comes out clean. Remove and cut into 1- by 3-inch slices. Return the cut cookie slices to the oven; bake again at 375 degrees for 10 minutes. Remove the biscotti from the oven, turn them over, and bake an additional 10 minutes. Turn the oven off, and leave the biscotti in for 1 to 2 hours to harden.

Yield: Approximately 40 biscotti

Orange Peanut Biscotti

2 ½ cups unbleached
   white flour
¼ cup vegetable oil
¼ cup water
1 Tbsp orange peel, grated

2 eggs
¼ cup honey
½ cup unsalted peanuts,
   chopped

In a large bowl, mix all the ingredients. Knead the dough on a lightly floured surface until firm. Separate the dough into two equal portions. Roll out the dough with a rolling pin to form a rectangle on a baking sheet, about 4½ to 5 inches by 11 to 12 inches. Repeat with the other piece of dough. Depending on the size of your baking sheet, both pieces of rolled-out dough should fit on the same baking sheet. Bake at 375 degrees for 30 to 35 minutes. Cookies are done when a toothpick inserted in the center comes out clean. Remove the cookies and cut into 1- by 3-inch slices. Return the cut cookie slices to the oven, and bake at 375 degrees for 10 minutes. Remove the biscotti from the oven, turn them over, and bake for 10 more minutes. Turn the oven off, and leave the biscotti in for 1 to 2 hours to harden.

Yield: Approximately 50 biscotti

Apple Sesame Biscotti

2 cups unbleached white
   flour
2 cups whole wheat flour
1/4 cup honey
1 Tbsp baking powder

1 cup all natural applesauce,
   no sugar added
2 eggs
1/2 cup water
1/4 cup sesame seeds

In a large bowl, mix all the ingredients. Knead the dough on a lightly floured surface until firm. Separate the dough into two equal portions. Roll out the dough with a rolling pin to form a rectangle on a baking sheet, about 4 1/2 to 5 inches by 11 to 12 inches. Repeat with the other piece of dough. Depending on the size of your baking sheet, both pieces of rolled-out dough should fit on the same baking sheet. Bake at 375 degrees for 30 to 35 minutes. Cookies are done when a toothpick inserted in the center comes out clean. Remove and cut into 1- by 3-inch slices. Return the cut cookie slices to the oven, and bake at 375 degrees for 10 minutes. Remove the biscotti from the oven, turn them over, and bake an additional 10 minutes. Turn the oven off, and leave the biscotti in for 1 to 2 hours to harden.

Yield: Approximately 70 biscotti

Plain Biscuits

½ cup powdered skim milk
1 egg
2 ½ cups unbleached white
    flour

½ tsp garlic powder
½ cup water
¼ cup vegetable oil

In a large bowl, mix all the ingredients. Knead the dough on a floured surface. Roll out the dough to ½-inch thickness, and cut out shapes with a cookie cutter. Put the biscuits on a baking sheet, ½ inch apart. Bake at 350 degrees for 25 to 30 minutes. When done, the biscuits should be firm to the touch. Turn the oven off, and leave the biscuits in for 1 to 2 hours to harden.

Yield: Approximately 50 two-inch biscuits

Whole Wheat Biscuits

2 ½ cups whole wheat
    flour
1 clove of garlic, crushed
1 egg

1 Tbsp honey
3 Tbsp vegetable oil
¾ cup water

In a large bowl, mix all the ingredients. Knead the dough on a lightly floured surface until firm. Roll out the dough to ¼-inch thickness, and cut out shapes with a cookie cutter. Put the cookies on a baking sheet, ½ inch apart. Bake at 300 degrees for 30 to 35 minutes. When done, the biscuits should be firm to the touch. Turn the oven off, and leave the biscuits in for 1 to 2 hours to harden.

Yield: Approximately 50 two-inch biscuits

Oats and Cheese Biscuits

1 cup quick-cooking oats, uncooked
¼ cup vegetable oil
1½ cups water
1 cup low-fat cheddar cheese, shredded
1 egg
3 cups whole wheat flour
¼ cup wheat germ

In a large bowl, mix all the ingredients. Knead the dough on a lightly floured surface until firm. Roll out the dough to ½-inch thickness, and cut out shapes with a cookie cutter. Put the biscuits on a baking sheet, ½ inch apart. Bake at 300 degrees for 55 to 60 minutes. When done, the biscuits should be firm to the touch. Turn the oven off, and leave the biscuits in for 1 to 2 hours to harden.

Yield: Approximately 75 two-inch biscuits

Chicken Biscuits

Ingredients

1 chicken leg, skin removed
1 ½ cups water
⅓ cup vegetable oil

1 egg
3 cups whole wheat flour

In a small pot, place the chicken and water. Bring to a boil, and simmer for 10 to 15 minutes or until the chicken is fully cooked. (Chicken is fully cooked when it is firm to the touch and there are no traces of blood in the joint area.) Set aside ¾ cup of the cooking water, and let it cool. In a large bowl, mix the other ingredients. Shred the chicken meat, and stir it into the flour. Add ¾ cup of the reserved chicken water to the flour mixture. Knead the dough on a floured surface until firm. Roll out the dough to ½-inch thickness, and cut out shapes with a cookie cutter. Put the cookies on a baking sheet, ½ inch apart. Bake at 325 degrees for 50 to 55 minutes. When done, the cookies should be firm to the touch. Turn the oven off, and leave the cookies in for 1 to 2 hours to harden.

Yield: Approximately 60 two-inch-long biscuits

Sunflower Seed Biscuits

3 cups whole wheat flour
½ cup unsalted and
    shelled sunflower seeds
½ tsp garlic powder

2 Tbsp vegetable oil
¼ cup all natural molasses
2 eggs
¾ cup water

In a large bowl, mix all the ingredients. Knead the dough on a floured surface. Let the dough sit for 30 minutes. Roll out the dough to ½-inch thickness, and cut out shapes with a cookie cutter. Put the biscuits on a baking sheet, 1 inch apart. Bake at 350 degrees for 30 to 35 minutes. When done, the biscuits should be golden in color and firm to the touch. Turn the oven off, and leave the biscuits in for 1 to 2 hours to harden.

Yield: Approximately 60 two-inch biscuits

Healthy Biscuits

2 cups whole wheat flour
1 egg yolk
2 tsp honey
2 tsp pure vanilla extract
2 Tbsp vegetable oil

1 Tbsp all natural
    molasses
1 Tbsp wheat germ
1 Tbsp powdered skim
    milk

In a large bowl, mix all the ingredients. Knead the dough on a floured surface until firm. Roll out the dough to ½-inch thickness. Cut into 1- by 2-inch strips. Place the strips on a baking sheet, 1 inch apart. Bake at 350 degrees for 15 to 20 minutes. When done, the biscuits should be firm to the touch. Turn the oven off, and leave the biscuits in for 1 to 2 hours to harden.

Yield: Approximately 40 two-inch biscuits

Garlic Biscuits

3 cups whole wheat flour	1 egg
$\frac{1}{4}$ tsp garlic powder	$\frac{3}{4}$ cup water

In a large bowl, mix all the ingredients. Knead the dough on a floured surface. Roll out the dough to $\frac{1}{4}$-inch thickness, and cut out shapes with a cookie cutter. Put the cookies on a baking sheet, $\frac{1}{2}$ inch apart. Bake at 350 degrees for 45 to 50 minutes. When done, the biscuits should be firm to the touch. Turn the oven off, and leave the biscuits in for 1 to 2 hours to harden.

Yield: Approximately 60 two-inch biscuits

Multigrain Chicken Biscuits

1 $\frac{1}{2}$ cups unbleached white flour	1 cup water
1 cup whole wheat flour	$\frac{1}{2}$ cup powdered skim milk
$\frac{1}{2}$ cup rye flour	1 egg
$\frac{1}{2}$ cup wheat germ	$\frac{1}{2}$ cup cooked chicken, with skin removed, shredded

In a large bowl, mix all the ingredients. Knead the dough on a floured surface. Roll out the dough to $\frac{1}{4}$-inch thickness, and cut out shapes with a cookie cutter. Put the biscuits on a baking sheet, $\frac{1}{2}$ inch apart. Bake at 300 degrees for 40 to 45 minutes. When done, the biscuits should be firm to the touch. Turn the oven off, and leave the biscuits in for 1 to 2 hours to harden.

Yield: Approximately 70 two-inch biscuits

Herb Biscuits

2 ½ cups whole wheat flour
1 ¼ cups cornmeal
2 tsp garlic powder
2 egg yolks
1 cup water

1 tsp dried parsley
1 tsp dried dill
1 tsp dried mint
1 tsp dried rosemary, crushed
1 tsp dried oregano

In a large bowl, mix all the ingredients. Knead the dough on a floured surface. Roll out the dough to ¼-inch thickness, and cut out shapes with a cookie cutter. Put the biscuits on a baking sheet, ½ inch apart. Bake at 375 degrees for 20 to 25 minutes. When done, the biscuits should be firm to the touch. Turn the oven off, and leave the biscuits in for 1 to 2 hours to harden.

Yield: Approximately 70 two-inch biscuits

Beef Biscuits

¾ cup water
3 cups unbleached white flour

¼ cup cooked lean beef, chopped and drained

In a large bowl, mix all the ingredients. Knead the dough on a floured surface. Roll out the dough to ¼-inch thickness, and cut out shapes with a cookie cutter. Put the biscuits on a baking sheet, ½ inch apart. Bake at 325 degrees for 45 to 50 minutes. When done, the biscuits should be firm to the touch. Turn the oven off, and leave the biscuits in for 1 to 2 hours to harden.

Yield: Approximately 60 two-inch biscuits

Cheddar Lover's Biscuits

Ingredients

2 cups unbleached white flour
½ cup low-fat cheddar cheese, shredded

2 garlic cloves, finely chopped
¼ cup vegetable oil
¼ cup water

In a large bowl, mix all the ingredients. Knead the dough on a floured surface. Roll out the dough to ½-inch thickness, and cut out shapes with a cookie cutter. Put the biscuits on a baking sheet, ½ inch apart. Bake at 400 degrees for 15 to 20 minutes. When done, the biscuits should be firm to the touch. Turn the oven off, and leave the biscuits in for 1 to 2 hours to harden.

Yield: Approximately 40 two-inch biscuits

Chicken and Cheese Biscuits

1 cup quick-cooking oats, uncooked
1/2 cup low-fat cheddar cheese, shredded
1/2 cup cooked chicken, chopped, with skin and bones removed
1 egg
1/2 cup wheat germ
1/4 cup vegetable oil
4 cups whole wheat flour
1 1/4 cups water

In a large bowl, mix all the ingredients. Knead the dough on a floured surface. Roll out the dough to 1/2-inch thickness, and cut out shapes with a cookie cutter. Put the biscuits on a baking sheet, 1/2 inch apart. Bake at 300 degrees for 55 to 60 minutes. When done, the biscuits should be firm to the touch. Turn the oven off, and leave the biscuits in for 1 to 2 hours to harden.

Yield: Approximately 90 two-inch biscuits

Honey Biscuits

2 1/2 cups whole wheat flour
2 eggs
1/3 cup honey
1/2 cup water

In a large bowl, mix all the ingredients. Knead the dough on a floured surface. Roll out the dough to 1/2-inch thickness, and cut out shapes with a cookie cutter. Put the biscuits on a baking sheet, 1/2 inch apart. Bake at 325 degrees for 15 to 20 minutes. When done, the biscuits should be firm to the touch. Turn the oven off, and leave the biscuits in for 1 to 2 hours to harden.

Yield: Approximately 50 two-inch biscuits

Sweet Potato Biscuits

4 cups whole wheat flour
2 cups cooked sweet potatoes,
   mashed

$\frac{1}{4}$ cup vegetable oil
$\frac{1}{2}$ cup milk
3 tsp baking powder

In a large bowl, mix all the ingredients. Knead the dough on a floured surface. Roll out the dough to $\frac{1}{2}$-inch thickness, and cut out shapes with a cookie cutter. Put the cookies on a baking sheet, $\frac{1}{2}$ inch apart. Bake at 400 degrees for 12 to 15 minutes. When done, the biscuits should be firm to the touch. Turn the oven off, and leave the biscuits in for 1 to 2 hours to harden.

Yield: Approximately 80 two-inch biscuits

Sunflower Bites

2 $\frac{1}{2}$ cups whole wheat
   flour
$\frac{1}{2}$ cup unsalted and
   shelled sunflower seeds

2 Tbsp vegetable oil
$\frac{1}{4}$ cup honey
$\frac{1}{4}$ cup cornmeal
$\frac{3}{4}$ cup water

In a large bowl, mix all the ingredients. Knead the dough on a lightly floured surface until firm. Roll out the dough to $\frac{1}{2}$-inch thickness, and cut out shapes with a cookie cutter. Put the cookies on a baking sheet, $\frac{1}{2}$ inch apart. Bake at 325 degrees for 40 to 45 minutes. When done, the cookies should be firm to the touch. Turn the oven off, and leave the cookies in for 1 to 2 hours to harden.

Yield: Approximately 50 two-inch cookies

Peanut Butter Bites

Ingredients

3 Tbsp vegetable oil
¼ cup all natural smooth peanut
    butter, no salt or sugar added
¼ cup honey

2 eggs
2 Tbsp water
2 cups whole wheat flour
1½ tsp baking powder

In a large bowl, mix all the ingredients well until the dough is stiff; if it is too sticky, mix in a small amount of flour. Knead the dough on a lightly floured surface until firm. Roll out the dough to ½-inch thickness, and cut out shapes with a cookie cutter. Put the cookies on a baking sheet, ½ inch apart. Bake at 350 degrees for 20 to 25 minutes. When done, the cookies should be firm to the touch. Turn the oven off, and leave the cookies in for 1 to 2 hours to harden.

Yield: Approximately 40 two-inch cookies

Cheese and Veggie Bites

Ingredients

2 ½ cups water
¼ cup celery, finely
   chopped
¼ cup carrots, chopped
2 cloves garlic, chopped
1 cup quick-cooking oats,
   uncooked

⅓ cup vegetable oil
½ cup low-fat cheddar
   cheese, shredded
1 egg
¼ cup wheat germ
3 cups whole wheat flour

In a small pot, place the water, celery, carrots, and garlic. Bring the vegetables to a boil, and simmer for 5 to 10 minutes to soften. Set the vegetables aside to cool. In a large bowl, mix the other ingredients. Add 1 ½ cups of the cooled vegetable water and the boiled vegetables to the flour mixture. Knead the dough on a floured surface until firm. Roll out the dough to ½-inch thickness, and cut out shapes with a cookie cutter. Put the cookies on a baking sheet, ½ inch apart. Bake at 325 degrees for 50 to 55 minutes. When done, the cookies should be firm to the touch. Turn the oven off, and leave the cookies in for 1 to 2 hours to harden.

Yield: Approximately 75 two-inch cookies

Barley Bites

1 1/4 cups barley flour
3 Tbsp vegetable oil

1/3 cup water

In a large bowl, mix all the ingredients. Knead the dough on a floured surface. Roll out the dough to 1/4-inch thickness, and cut out shapes with a cookie cutter. Put the cookies on a baking sheet, 1/2 inch apart. With a knife, score the dough. Bake at 350 degrees for 15 to 20 minutes. When done, the cookies should be firm to the touch. Turn the oven off, and leave the cookies in for 1 to 2 hours to harden.

Yield: Approximately 25 two-inch cookies

Wheat Germ Lemon Bites

1 3/4 cups whole wheat flour
1/4 cup honey
1 Tbsp grated lemon rind
1 egg yolk
2 Tbsp wheat germ

1/4 cup sesame seeds
1/2 cup vegetable oil
1/2 cup unsalted peanuts, chopped
2 Tbsp pure vanilla extract

In a large bowl, mix all the ingredients. Knead the dough on a floured surface. Roll out the dough to 1/2-inch thickness, and cut out shapes with a cookie cutter. Put the cookies on a baking sheet, 1/2 inch apart. Bake at 375 degrees for 15 to 20 minutes. When done, the cookies should be firm to the touch. Turn the oven off, and leave the cookies in for 1 to 2 hours to harden.

Yield: Approximately 35 two-inch cookies

Kooper's Rice Bones

2 cups whole wheat flour
2 cups rice flour
1 egg
½ cup water

½ cup vegetable oil
¼ cup all natural peanut
butter, no salt or
sugar added

In a large bowl, mix all the ingredients. Knead the dough on a floured surface. Roll out the dough to ¼-inch thickness, and cut out shapes with a dog bone cookie cutter. Put the cookies on a baking sheet, ½ inch apart. Bake at 350 degrees for 15 to 20 minutes. When done, the cookies should be firm to the touch. Turn the oven off, and leave the cookies in for 1 to 2 hours to harden.

Yield: Approximately 80 two-inch cookies

Oatmeal Bones

1 egg
½ cup vegetable oil
½ cup water

2 cups whole wheat flour
1 ½ cups quick-cooking
oats, uncooked

In a large bowl, mix all the ingredients. Knead the dough on a floured surface. Roll out the dough to ½-inch thickness, and cut out shapes with a dog bone cookie cutter. Put the cookies on a baking sheet, 1 inch apart. Bake at 350 degrees for 25 to 30 minutes. When done, the cookies should be firm to the touch. Turn the oven off, and leave the cookies in for 1 to 2 hours to harden.

Yield: Approximately 60 two-inch cookies

Turkey Bones

Ingredients

2 cups whole wheat flour
½ cup wheat germ
1 cup cooked turkey, chopped,
   with all bones removed

1 egg
½ cup vegetable oil
½ cup water

In a large bowl, mix all the ingredients. Knead the dough on a floured surface. Roll out the dough to ½-inch thickness, and cut out shapes with a dog bone cookie cutter. Put the cookies on a baking sheet, 1 inch apart. Bake at 350 degrees for 25 to 30 minutes. When done, the cookies should be firm to the touch. Turn the oven off, and leave the cookies in for 1 to 2 hours to harden.

For variations, substitute the turkey with:
1 cup cooked lean beef, chopped, with all bones removed
1 cup cooked skinless chicken, chopped, with all bones removed
1 cup powdered skim milk
1 cup cooked peas and carrots, mashed

Yield: Approximately 40 two-inch cookies

Ham and Swiss Bones

½ cup low-sodium Swiss
  cheese, shredded
½ cup low-sodium ham,
  chopped

2 ½ cups rye flour
⅓ cup vegetable oil
1 egg
½ cup water

In a large bowl, mix all the ingredients. Knead the dough on a floured surface. Roll out the dough to ½-inch thickness, and cut out shapes with a dog bone cookie cutter. Put the cookies on a baking sheet, 1 inch apart. Bake at 350 degrees for 25 to 30 minutes. When done, the cookies should be firm to the touch. Turn the oven off, and leave the cookies in for 1 to 2 hours to harden.

Yield: Approximately 50 two-inch cookies

Liver Oatmeal Bones

Ingredients

$^1/_4$ cup freeze-dried liver☙
4 cups whole wheat flour
1 cup quick-cooking oats,
    uncooked
1 cup rye flour

1 egg
$^1/_2$ cup vegetable oil
1 $^3/_4$ cups water
1 tsp garlic powder

Place the liver cubes in a blender, and blend to a powder. In a large bowl, mix all the ingredients. Knead the dough on a floured surface. Roll out the dough to $^1/_2$-inch thickness, and cut out shapes with a dog bone cookie cutter. Put the cookies on a baking sheet, $^1/_2$ inch apart. Bake at 325 degrees for 35 to 40 minutes. When done, the cookies should be firm to the touch. Turn the oven off, and leave the cookies in for 1 to 2 hours to harden.

Yield: Approximately 110 two-inch cookies
☙Available at pet stores

My Honey Boy Bones

$^3/_4$ cup water

$^1/_4$ cup vegetable oil

$^1/_2$ cup powdered skim milk

2 tsp honey

1 egg

3 cups whole wheat flour

In a large bowl, mix all the ingredients. Knead the dough on a floured surface. Roll out the dough to $^1/_2$-inch thickness, and cut out shapes with a dog bone cookie cutter. Put the cookies on a baking sheet, $^1/_2$ inch apart. Bake at 325 degrees for 40 to 45 minutes. When done, the cookies should be firm to the touch. Turn the oven off, and leave the cookies in for 1 to 2 hours to harden.

Yield: Approximately 60 two-inch cookies

Garlic and Cheese Bones

2 cups whole wheat flour

$^1/_2$ cup low-fat cheddar cheese, shredded

$^1/_2$ tsp garlic powder

$^1/_2$ cup vegetable oil

$^1/_4$ cup water

In a large bowl, mix all the ingredients. Knead the dough on a floured surface. Roll out the dough to $^1/_2$-inch thickness, and cut out shapes with a dog bone cookie cutter. Put the cookies on a baking sheet, $^1/_2$ inch apart. Bake at 400 degrees for 10 to 15 minutes. When done, the cookies should be firm to the touch. Turn the oven off, and leave the cookies in for 1 to 2 hours to harden.

Yield: Approximately 40 two-inch cookies

Red Bones

¼ cup freeze-dried liver🐾
1 cup water
½ cup all natural tomato juice, no
    salt added

3 ½ cups unbleached white flour
1 cup wheat germ

Place freeze-dried liver chunks in a blender, and blend to a powder. In a large bowl, mix all the ingredients. Knead the dough on a floured surface. Roll out the dough to ¼-inch thickness, and cut out shapes with a dog bone cookie cutter. Put the cookies on a baking sheet, ½ inch apart. Bake at 350 degrees for 35 to 40 minutes. When done, the cookies should be firm to the touch. Turn the oven off, and leave the cookies in for 1 to 2 hours to harden.

Yield: Approximately 80 two-inch cookies
🐾Available at pet stores

Fish Bones

1 cup cornmeal
1 cup quick-cooking oats,
    uncooked
¼ tsp baking powder

1 Tbsp garlic powder
6 oz canned tuna in
    water, drained and
    rinsed

In a large bowl, mix all the ingredients. Knead the dough on a floured surface. Roll out the dough to ¼-inch thickness, and cut out shapes with a dog bone cookie cutter. Put the cookies on a baking sheet, ½ inch apart. Bake at 350 degrees for 25 to 30 minutes. When done, the cookies should be firm to the touch. Turn the oven off, and leave the cookies in for 1 to 2 hours to harden.

Yield: Approximately 40 two-inch cookies

Grinder Bones

Ingredients

1 Tbsp freeze-dried liver 🐾
3 ½ cups rye flour
¾ cup powdered skim milk
1 Tbsp garlic powder
1 tsp bone meal ❤

1 Tbsp chopped fresh parsley
　or ½ tsp dried parsley
⅓ cup vegetable oil
¾ cup water
1 egg

Place the liver cubes in a blender, and blend to a powder. In a large bowl, mix all the ingredients. Knead the dough on a floured surface. Roll out the dough to ½-inch thickness, and cut out shapes with a dog bone cookie cutter. Put the cookies on a baking sheet, ½ inch apart. Bake at 350 degrees for 35 to 40 minutes. When done, the cookies should be firm to the touch. Turn the oven off, and leave the cookies in for 1 to 2 hours to harden.

Yield: Approximately 70 two-inch cookies
🐾 Available at pet stores
❤ Available at health food stores and some grocery stores

Salad Bones

Ingredients

Dough
½ cup of mixed vegetables (carrots, peas, celery, broccoli)
1 egg yolk

½ cup water
2 Tbsp vegetable oil
2 cups whole wheat flour

Topping
1 egg white
1 Tbsp dried parsley

1 Tbsp dried oregano

Put the vegetable mix in a blender with the egg yolk, water, and oil. Blend to the consistency of a thick vegetable juice. Put the flour in a large bowl, and add the vegetables. Mix well. If the mixture is too dry, add a small amount of water; if too wet, add more flour. (This will depend on the vegetables used and whether they are fresh or frozen.) Knead the dough on a floured surface. Roll out the dough to ¼-inch thickness, and cut out shapes with a dog bone cookie cutter. Put the cookies on a baking sheet, ½ inch apart. Mix together all the topping ingredients, and brush the mixture on the dough. Bake at 375 degrees for 20 minutes. When done, the cookies should be firm to the touch. Turn the oven off, and leave the cookies in for 1 to 2 hours to harden.

Yield: Approximately 40 two-inch cookies

Peanut Butter Carob Chip Bones

2 ½ cups unbleached white flour
½ cup carob chips
¾ cup all natural smooth peanut
   butter, no salt or sugar added

1 egg
¼ cup vegetable oil
¾ cup water
½ cup wheat germ

In a large bowl, mix all the ingredients. Knead the dough on a floured surface. Roll out the dough to ½-inch thickness, and cut out shapes with a dog bone cookie cutter. Put the cookies on a baking sheet, ½ inch apart. Bake at 350 degrees for 30 to 35 minutes. When done, the cookies should be firm to the touch. Turn the oven off, and leave the cookies in for 1 to 2 hours to harden.

Yield: Approximately 55 two-inch cookies

Available at health food stores and some grocery stores

Oatmeal and Cheese Bones

1 cup quick-cooking oats, uncooked
4 Tbsp vegetable oil
1 $\frac{1}{3}$ cups water
$\frac{1}{2}$ cup powdered skim milk
$\frac{1}{2}$ cup low-fat cheddar cheese, shredded

1 egg
1 cup cornmeal
$\frac{1}{2}$ cup wheat germ
3 $\frac{1}{2}$ cups whole wheat
   flour

In a large bowl, mix all the ingredients. Knead the dough on a floured surface. Roll out the dough to $\frac{1}{2}$-inch thickness, and cut out shapes with a dog bone cookie cutter. Put the cookies on a baking sheet, $\frac{1}{2}$ inch apart. Bake at 300 degrees for 55 to 60 minutes. When done, the cookies should be firm to the touch. Turn the oven off, and leave the cookies in for 1 to 2 hours to harden.

Yield: Approximately 100 two-inch cookies

Brown Rice with Parsley Cookies

2 $\frac{1}{2}$ cups whole wheat flour
$\frac{1}{4}$ tsp garlic powder
3 Tbsp dried parsley leaves

1 cup brown rice, cooked
3 Tbsp vegetable oil
$\frac{3}{4}$ cup water

In a large bowl, mix all the ingredients. Knead the dough on a lightly floured surface until firm. Roll out the dough to $\frac{1}{4}$-inch thickness, and cut out shapes with a cookie cutter. Put the cookies on a baking sheet, $\frac{1}{2}$ inch apart. Bake at 350 degrees for 25 to 30 minutes. When done, the cookies should be firm to the touch. Turn the oven off, and leave the cookies in for 1 to 2 hours to harden.

Yield: Approximately 65 two-inch cookies

Cheese Braids

Ingredients

3 ½ cups whole wheat flour
½ cup low-fat cheddar cheese, shredded
¼ cup Parmesan cheese, grated

1 egg
1 cup skim milk
¼ cup vegetable oil

In a large bowl, mix all the ingredients. Knead the dough on a floured surface. Roll out the dough to 1/2-inch thickness. Cut into ½- by 3-inch strips. Pinch together the tips of two strips. Place the strips on a baking sheet. Braid two strips of dough, pinching the ends into baking sheet. Repeat until all the dough is used. Bakeat 350 degrees for 30 to 35 minutes. When done, the cookies should be firm to the touch. Turn the oven off, and leave the cookies in for 1 to 2 hours to harden.

Yield: Approximately 45 cookies

Carob Chip Cookies

Ingredients

½ cup carob chips
2 ¾ cups whole wheat flour
1 tsp baking powder

¼ cup vegetable oil
¼ cup honey
¾ cup water

Melt the carob chips in a double boiler over low heat, stirring until melted. With a spatula, transfer the melted carob to a large bowl, and let it cool to room temperature. Add the other ingredients, and mix well. Divide the dough in half, and wrap it in plastic wrap. Chill until firm, about 1 hour. On a floured surface, roll out the dough to ¼-inch thickness. Cut out shapes with a cookie cutter. Put the cookies on a baking sheet, 1 inch apart. Bake at 350 degrees for 8 to 10 minutes. When done, the cookies should be firm to the touch. Turn the oven off, and leave the cookies in for 1 to 2 hours to harden.

Yield: Approximately 55 two-inch cookies
🐾Available at health food stores and some grocery stores

Peanut Butter Banana Cookies

3 cups whole wheat flour

1 egg

1 banana, mashed

¼ cup all natural peanut butter, no salt or sugar added

¾ cup water

In a large bowl, mix all the ingredients. Knead the dough on a floured surface until firm. Roll out the dough to ¼-inch thickness, and cut out shapes with a cookie cutter. Put the cookies on a baking sheet, ½ inch apart. Bake at 350 degrees for 40 to 45 minutes. When done, the cookies should be firm to the touch. Turn the oven off, and leave the cookies in for 1 to 2 hours to harden.

Yield: Approximately 60 two-inch cookies

Almond Cookies

1 ½ cups whole wheat flour

½ tsp pure almond extract

1 egg

¼ cup honey

¼ cup vegetable oil

In a large bowl, mix all the ingredients. Knead the dough on a floured surface until firm. Roll out the dough to ½-inch thickness, and cut out shapes with a cookie cutter. Put the cookies on a baking sheet, ½ inch apart. Bake at 375 degrees for 10 to 15 minutes. When done, the cookies should be firm to the touch. Turn the oven off, and leave the cookies in for 1 to 2 hours to harden.

Yield: Approximately 30 two-inch cookies

Carob Nut Cookies

Ingredients

Cookie Dough

5 cups rice flour
1 tsp baking powder
½ cup carob chips
1 egg
¼ cup honey
½ cup all natural peanut butter, no salt or sugar added
½ cup all natural applesauce, no sugar added
½ cup vegetable oil
2 tsp pure vanilla extract
1½ cups water

Toppings

⅓ cup quick-cooking oats, uncooked
⅓ cup unsalted peanuts, chopped
⅓ cup carob chips, chopped

In a large bowl, mix all the ingredients for the cookie dough. On a lightly floured surface, knead the dough until firm. Roll out the dough to ¼-inch thickness. Sprinkle toppings over the dough. With a rolling pin or your hands, gently press the toppings into the dough. Cut out shapes with a cookie cutter, and put them on a baking sheet, 1 inch apart. Bake at 325 degrees for 20 to 25 minutes. When done, the cookies should be firm to the touch. Turn the oven off, and leave the cookies in for 1 to 2 hours to harden.

Yield: Approximately 100 two-inch cookies
Available at health food stores and some grocery stores

Apple Cinnamon Delights

4 cups unbleached white flour
½ cup all natural applesauce, no sugar added
½ cup vegetable oil
¼ cup honey

¾ cup water
2 eggs
¼ cup wheat germ
1 Tbsp ground cinnamon
1 tsp baking soda

In a large bowl, mix all ingredients. Knead the dough on a floured surface. Roll out the dough to ½-inch thickness, and cut out shapes with a cookie cutter. Put the cookies on a baking sheet, 1 inch apart. Bake at 400 degrees for 8 to 10 minutes. When done, the cookies should be firm to the touch. Turn the oven off, and leave the cookies in for 1 to 2 hours to harden.

Yield: Approximately 80 two-inch cookies

Wheat Germ Carob Cookies

3 cups whole wheat flour
$\frac{1}{2}$ cup wheat germ
2 $\frac{1}{2}$ cups quick-cooking oats, uncooked
1 Tbsp honey

$\frac{1}{4}$ cup vegetable oil
$\frac{1}{4}$ cup carob chips, melted
$\frac{1}{4}$ cup all natural molasses
1 cup water
$\frac{1}{2}$ cup skim milk

In a large bowl, mix all the ingredients. Knead the dough on a floured surface. Roll out the dough to $\frac{1}{2}$-inch thickness, and cut out shapes with a cookie cutter. Put the cookies on a baking sheet, $\frac{1}{2}$ inch apart. Bake at 350 degrees for 40 to 45 minutes. When done, the cookies should be firm to the touch. Turn the oven off, and leave the cookies in for 1 to 2 hours to harden.

Yield: Approximately 100 two-inch cookies

Bran and Peanut Butter Oatmeal Cookies

Ingredients

4 ½ cups whole wheat flour
½ cup bran flake cereal, no sugar added
½ cup quick-cooking oats, uncooked
2 eggs

1 cup skim milk
½ cup all natural peanut butter, no sugar or salt added
¼ cup honey
¼ cup water

In a large bowl, mix all the ingredients. Knead the dough on a floured surface. Roll out the dough to ½-inch thickness, and cut out shapes with a cookie cutter. Put the cookies on a baking sheet, ½ inch apart. Bake at 350 degrees for 20 to 25 minutes. When done, the cookies should be firm to the touch. Turn the oven off, and leave the cookies in for 1 to 2 hours to harden.

Yield: Approximately 100 two-inch cookies

Rice and Cheese Cookies

1 ¼ cups water
½ cup powdered skim milk
½ cup low-fat cheddar
    cheese, shredded

2 eggs
1 tsp garlic powder
4 cups rice flour

In a large bowl, mix all the ingredients. Knead the dough on a floured surface. Roll out the dough to ¼-inch thickness, and cut out shapes with a cookie cutter. Put the cookies on a baking sheet, ½ inch apart. Bake at 350 degrees for 15 to 20 minutes. When done, the cookies should be firm to the touch. Turn the oven off, and leave the cookies in for 1 to 2 hours to harden.

Yield: Approximately 80 two-inch cookies

Sweet Potato Cookies

¼ cup vegetable oil
2 ½ cups unbleached
    white flour
1 cup cooked sweet
    potatoes, mashed
2 eggs

1 tsp pure vanilla extract
½ cup unsalted walnuts,
    chopped
½ cup water
¼ cup honey

In a large bowl, mix all the ingredients. Knead the dough on a floured surface. Roll out the dough to ½-inch thickness, and cut out shapes with a cookie cutter. Put the cookies on a baking sheet, ½ inch apart. Bake at 350 degrees for 15 to 20 minutes. When done, the cookies should be firm to the touch. Turn the oven off, and leave the cookies in for 1 to 2 hours to harden.

Yield: Approximately 45 two-inch cookies

Peanut Butter Carob Cookies

6 Tbsp all natural applesauce, no sugar added
¼ cup honey
½ cup vegetable oil
½ cup all natural peanut butter, no salt or sugar added
1 tsp pure vanilla extract

1 ½ cups unbleached white flour
1 cup whole wheat flour
½ cup carob powderd
2 eggs
1 Tbsp ground cinnamon
2 tsp baking soda

In a large bowl, mix all the ingredients. With your hands, make 1-inch balls with the dough. Place the balls 3 inches apart on a baking sheet. With a fork, flatten each ball, leaving indent marks from the fork. Bake at 350 degrees for 10 to 12 minutes. When done, the cookies should be firm to the touch. Turn the oven off, and leave the cookies in for 1 to 2 hours to harden.

Yield: Approximately 55 cookies
🐾 Available at health food stores and some grocery stores

Carob and Mint Delights

2 cups whole wheat flour
1 cup quick-cooking oats,
   uncooked
1 cup fresh mint leaves, chopped,
   or $\frac{1}{2}$ cup dried mint leaves

$\frac{1}{2}$ cup wheat germ
$\frac{1}{2}$ cup carob chips🐾
$\frac{1}{4}$ cup water
1 cup skim milk
1 cup unbleached white flour

In a large bowl, mix all the ingredients. Knead the dough on a floured surface. Roll out the dough to $\frac{1}{2}$-inch thickness, and cut out shapes with a cookie cutter. Put the cookies on a baking sheet, $\frac{1}{2}$ inch apart. Bake at 350 degrees for 35 to 40 minutes. When done, the cookies should be firm to the touch. Turn the oven off, and leave the cookies in for 1 to 2 hours to harden.

Yield: Approximately 75 two-inch cookies
🐾 Available at health food stores and some grocery stores

Rye Crisps

1 $\frac{1}{2}$ cups rye flour
3 Tbsp vegetable oil

$\frac{1}{4}$ tsp garlic powder
$\frac{1}{3}$ cup water

In a large bowl, mix all the ingredients. Knead the dough on a floured surface until firm. Roll out the dough to $\frac{1}{4}$-inch thickness. Cut into 2-inch squares. Put the crisps on a baking sheet, 1 inch apart. Bake at 350 degrees for 15 to 20 minutes. When done, the crisps should be golden in color and firm to the touch. Turn the oven off, and leave the crisps in for 1 to 2 hours to harden.

Yield: Approximately 30 two-inch crisps

Sesame and Cheese Sticks

Ingredients

1 ½ cups whole wheat flour
¼ cup vegetable oil
¼ cup water

1 egg
½ cup Parmesan cheese
½ cup sesame seeds

Combine the flour, oil, and water to make a firm dough. Knead the dough on a floured surface. Roll out the dough in a rectangle, ¼ inch thick. Lightly beat the egg, and brush it on the dough. Sprinkle the surface with cheese and sesame seeds. With a rolling pin, lightly roll over the surface to push the cheese and sesame seeds into the dough, or press the ingredients firmly with your hands. Cut the dough lengthwise into 1- by 2-inch strips. Place the strips ½ inch apart on a baking sheet. Twist each strip twice, and press the ends into baking sheet; this will prevent the dough from untwisting. Bake at 400 degrees for 12 to 15 minutes or until golden brown. Turn the oven off, and leave the sticks in for 1 to 2 hours to harden.

Yield: Approximately 30 two-inch-long sticks

Cheddar Cheese Sticks

2 cups whole wheat flour
½ tsp baking powder
½ cup low-fat cheddar cheese,
    shredded

¼ cup vegetable oil
⅓ cup water

In a large bowl, mix all the ingredients. Knead the dough on a floured surface until firm. Roll out the dough to ¼-inch thickness. Cut into ½- by 2-inch strips. Put the cookies on a baking sheet, ½ inch apart. Bake at 400 degrees for 10 to 15 minutes. When done, the sticks should be golden brown and firm to the touch. Turn the oven off, and leave the sticks in for 1 to 2 hours to harden.

Yield: Approximately 40 two-inch sticks

Liver Parsley Treats

½ cup freeze-dried
    liver🐾
2 Tbsp fresh parsley,
    chopped or 1 Tbsp
    dried parsley

2 cups whole wheat flour
½ cup wheat germ
⅓ cup water
3 Tbsp vegetable oil
1 egg

Place the liver cubes in a blender, and blend to a powder. In a large bowl, mix all the ingredients. Knead the dough on a floured surface. Roll out the dough to ½-inch thickness, and cut out shapes with a cookie cutter. Put the cookies on a baking sheet, ½ inch apart. Bake at 400 degrees for 15 to 17 minutes. When done, the treats should be firm to the touch. Turn the oven off, and leave the treats in for 1 to 2 hours to harden.

Yield: Approximately 40 two-inch treats
🐾 Available at pet food stores

Liver and Garlic Strips

½ lb liver
2 eggs
½ cup water

2 cups whole wheat
flour
1 Tbsp garlic powder

In a blender, mix the liver, eggs, and water. Add the remaining ingredients, and mix well. Pour into a 9- by 12- by 2-inch baking pan, and spread the mixture evenly in the pan. Bake at 350 degrees for 35 to 40 minutes. When done, the mixture should be dry on top and firm to the touch. Cool the mixture in the pan, and then cut it into 1- by 2-inch strips.

Yield: Approximately 50 strips

Bars

Basic Granola Recipe

Ingredients

1 ½ cups quick-cooking oats, uncooked
½ cup wheat germ

¼ cup honey
2 tsp vegetable oil

In a large bowl, mix all the ingredients except the wheat germ. Sprinkle the wheat germ on a baking sheet. Spread the oat mixture on top of the wheat germ; do not try to spread the mixture over the entire baking sheet. (I find it is easier to spread the mixture into small 3- by 3-inch sections over the baking sheet.) Bake at 325 degrees for 25 to 30 minutes. Check the pieces as they bake; after 10 minutes, turn them over. Continue baking for the remaining 15 to 20 minutes until the pieces are hard and golden brown. Cool on a baking rack. Store in a covered container or plastic storage bag in the refrigerator. (I normally put the pieces in a plastic storage bag and crush them with a rolling pin; then I sprinkle the granola over frozen treats, use it for granola bars, and use it to decorate cakes or muffins.)

Yield: Approximately 2 cups

Granola Bars

Ingredients

³/₄ cup quick-cooking oats, uncooked

¹/₄ cup whole wheat flour

¹/₂ cup granola, crushed (see basic recipe, page 56)

¹/₃ cup plus 1 Tbsp honey

¹/₄ cup vegetable oil

1 egg

¹/₄ tsp pure vanilla extract

In a large bowl, mix the oats, flour, granola, ¹/₃ cup of honey, and oil. Blend well. In a separate bowl, beat the egg, vanilla, and remaining 1 Tbsp honey. Add the wet mixture to the oatmeal mixture, and mix together. Spread evenly over a well-greased and floured 9- by 9- by 2-inch baking pan. Bake at 325 degrees for 30 to 35 minutes. The granola should be firm and dry to the touch. Cool slightly, and cut into bars of desired size. Store in a covered container or plastic storage bag in the refrigerator.

Yield: Approximately 40 bars

Carob Chip Bars

¼ cup vegetable oil

½ cup all natural applesauce, no sugar added

¼ cup honey

1 tsp pure vanilla extract

1 egg

1½ cups unbleached white flour

1 cup carob chips

½ cup unsalted walnuts, chopped

In a medium bowl, mix all the wet ingredients. In a large bowl, mix all the dry ingredients. Slowly add the wet ingredients to the dry mixture, and mix well. Pour the batter into a greased 9- by 13- by 2-inch baking pan. Bake at 375 degrees for 20 to 25 minutes. The bars are done when a toothpick inserted in the center comes out clean. Cool and cut into 1½-inch squares.

Yield: Approximately 54 bars

Available at health food stores and some grocery stores

Banana Apple Sour Cream Bars

1 egg
⅓ cup all natural applesauce, no
    sugar added
¼ cup honey
1 banana, cut into small chunks

1½ cups unbleached white flour
1 tsp baking soda
¼ cup sour cream
½ tsp pure vanilla extract
½ cup unsalted walnuts, chopped

In a large bowl, mix all the ingredients well. Pour the batter into a greased 9- by 13- by 2-inch baking pan. Bake at 350 degrees for 40 to 45 minutes. The bars are done when a toothpick inserted in the center comes out clean. Cool and cut into 1½-inch squares.

Yield: Approximately 54 bars

Apple Bars

½ cup all natural apple-
    sauce, no sugar added
¼ cup honey
1 egg
1 cup whole wheat flour

½ tsp baking powder
1 apple, chopped, skin
    and core removed
½ cup unsalted peanuts,
    chopped

In a large bowl, mix all the ingredients with a spoon. Grease and line an 8- by 8- by 2-inch baking pan with wax paper. Spread the mixture evenly in the pan. Bake at 325 degrees for 30 to 35 minutes. The bars are done when the edges are browned. Cool, turn out on wire rack, remove the wax paper, and cut into bars.

Yield: Approximately 22 bars

Cheddar Bars

Ingredients

⅓ cup all natural applesauce, no sugar added

⅓ cup low-fat cheddar cheese, shredded

⅓ cup water

2 cups unbleached white flour

In a medium bowl, mix all the wet ingredients. In a large bowl, mix all the dry ingredients. Slowly add the wet ingredients to the dry mixture, and mix well. Pour the batter into a greased 9- by 13-inch baking pan. Bake at 375 degrees for 25 to 30 minutes. The bars are done when a toothpick inserted in the center comes out clean. Cool and cut into 1 ½-inch bars.

Yield: Approximately 54 bars

Carob Oatmeal Bars

¼ cup vegetable oil

¼ cup honey

2 eggs

½ tsp pure vanilla extract

¼ cup water

1 cup whole wheat flour

½ tsp baking powder

2 cups quick-cooking oats, uncooked

¾ cup carob chips

In a medium bowl, mix all the wet ingredients. In a large bowl, mix all the dry ingredients. Slowly add the wet ingredients to the dry mixture, and mix well. Pour the batter into a greased 9-inch square baking pan. Bake at 350 degrees for 30 to 35 minutes. The bars are done when a toothpick inserted in the center comes out clean. Cool and cut into 2-inch-square bars.

Yield: Approximately 16 bars

Available at health food stores and some grocery stores

Fruit Bars

Ingredients

2 cups whole wheat flour
¼ cup honey
1 tsp lemon rind, grated
¼ tsp ground nutmeg
¼ tsp ground cinnamon

½ cup vegetable oil
1 ¼ cups of fruit, with skin, pits, and core removed

Put the fruit in a blender and puree, leaving the mixture firm. If it is too runny, add small amounts of flour until it is firm. Set aside the puree mixture.

Mix all the other ingredients in a separate bowl; this mixture should be crumbly. Set aside 1 cup of the flour mixture. Pat the remaining mixture into a greased 9- by 9- by 2-inch baking pan. Spread the puree mixture evenly over the top of the dough, leaving a ¼-inch border around the edges. Sprinkle the reserved flour mixture over the puree. Bake at 375 degrees for 35 to 40 minutes. The bars are done when the puree is firm and holds its firmness when cut; the mixture should be dry and firm to the touch. Cool completely and cut into 2-inch squares.

Yield: Approximately 16 bars

Power Bars

1 cup quick-cooking oats, uncooked

$\frac{1}{2}$ cup whole wheat flour

2 Tbsp vegetable oil

$\frac{1}{2}$ cup wheat germ

$\frac{1}{4}$ cup honey

$\frac{1}{2}$ tsp ground ginger

1 egg

$\frac{1}{3}$ cup all natural apple-sauce, no sugar added

$\frac{1}{2}$ cup raisins

$\frac{1}{2}$ cup carob chips

$\frac{1}{4}$ cup unsalted and shelled sunflower seeds

$\frac{1}{4}$ cup unsalted walnuts, chopped

In a large bowl, mix all the ingredients with a spoon. Grease and line an 8- by 8- by 2-inch baking pan with wax paper. Spread the mixture evenly in the pan. Bake at 325 degrees for 30 to 35 minutes. The bars are done when the edges are browned. Cool, turn out on wire rack, remove the wax paper, and cut into 2-inch squares.

Yield: Approximately 22 bars

❖ Available at health food stores and some grocery stores

Cream Cheese Carob Bars

Ingredients

⅓ cup all natural apple-
   sauce, no sugar added
¼ cup honey
1 tsp pure vanilla extract
8 oz cream cheese,
   softened

2 eggs
1 cup unbleached white
   flour
½ cup unsalted walnuts,
   chopped
½ cup carob chips🐾

In a medium bowl, mix all the wet ingredients. In a large bowl, mix all the dry
ingredients. Slowly add the wet ingredients to
the dry mixture, and mix well. Pour the batter
into a greased 9- by 13- by 2-inch baking pan. Bake
at 350 degrees for 35 to 40 minutes. The bars are
done when a toothpick inserted in the center comes
out clean. Cool and cut into 2-inch squares.

Yield: Approximately 28 bars
🐾Available at health food stores and some grocery stores

Sour Cream Apple Squares

Ingredients

¼ cup sour cream

½ cup all natural applesauce, no
  sugar added

1 tsp pure vanilla extract

¼ cup honey

2 Tbsp vegetable oil

1 egg

2 ¼ cups unbleached white flour

1 tsp ground cinnamon

1 tsp baking soda

¼ cup unsalted walnuts,
  chopped

In a medium bowl, mix all the wet ingredients. In a large bowl, mix all the dry ingredients. Press the dry mixture into the bottom of a greased 9- by 13- by 2-inch baking pan. Pour the wet ingredients evenly over the packed dry ingredients. Bake at 350 degrees for 30 to 35 minutes. The bars are done when a toothpick inserted in the center comes out clean. Cool and cut into 2-inch squares.

Yield: Approximately 28 squares

Carob Squares

Dough

4 ½ cups whole wheat flour

1 egg

¼ cup carob powderd

1 ¼ cups water

Frosting

8 oz low-fat cream cheese, softened

1 Tbsp pure vanilla extract

2 Tbsp honey

¼ cup vegetable oil

In a large bowl, mix the ingredients for the dough. Knead the dough on a lightly floured surface. Roll out the dough to ¼-inch thickness. Cut the dough into 2-inch squares. Place the squares on a baking sheet. Bake at 350 degrees for 35 to 40 minutes. The squares are done when a toothpick inserted in the center comes out clean. Set aside to cool. Mix all the ingredients for the frosting until smooth. Frost the cooled bars.

Yield: Approximately 70 squares

🐾Available at health food stores and some grocery stores

Drop Cookies

Banana Oatmeal Cookies

Ingredients

1 ½ cups unbleached white
flour

½ tsp baking soda

¼ tsp ground nutmeg

½ tsp ground cinnamon

1 cup all natural apple-
sauce, no sugar added

¼ cup vegetable oil

3 bananas, mashed

¼ cup honey

1 ¾ cups quick-cooking
oats, uncooked

¼ cup unsalted walnuts,
chopped

In a large bowl, mix all the ingredients. With a teaspoon, drop spoonfuls of dough on a baking sheet, about 1 ½ inches apart. Bake at 350 degrees or 10 to 15 minutes. When done, the cookies should be firm to the touch. Turn the oven off, and leave the cookies in for 1 to 2 hours to harden.

Yield: Approximately 55 cookies

Peanut Butter Oatmeal Cookies

½ cup water
¼ cup vegetable oil
¼ cup honey
½ cup all natural chunky
    peanut butter, no salt or
    sugar added

1 tsp pure vanilla extract
1 egg
1½ cups whole wheat flour
¾ cup quick-cooking oats,
    uncooked

In a large bowl, mix all the ingredients. With a teaspoon, drop spoonfuls of dough on a baking sheet, about 1 inch apart. Bake at 350 degrees for about 15 to 18 minutes. When done, the cookies should be firm to the touch. Turn the oven off, and leave the cookies in for 1 to 2 hours to harden.

Yield: Approximately 45 cookies

Cream Cheese Carob Cookies

8 oz cream cheese, softened
2½ cups whole wheat flour
1 tsp baking powder
1 cup all natural applesauce,
    no sugar added

¼ cup honey
1 egg
1 tsp pure vanilla extract
½ cup carob chips*

In a large bowl, mix all the ingredients. With a teaspoon, drop spoonfuls of dough on a baking sheet, about 1½ inches apart. Bake at 375 degrees for 15 to 20 minutes. When done, the cookies should be firm to the touch. Turn the oven off, and leave the cookies in for 1 to 2 hours to harden.

Yield: Approximately 50 cookies
🐾Available at health food stores and some grocery stores

Peanut Butter Apple Cookies

1 apple, chopped, with skin and core removed
$1/3$ cup vegetable oil
$1/4$ cup all natural peanut butter, no salt or sugar added
$1/4$ cup honey
1 egg
2 cups whole wheat flour
$1/2$ cup water

In a large bowl, mix all the ingredients. With a teaspoon, drop spoonfuls of dough onto a baking sheet, 1 inch apart. Bake at 350 degrees for 12 to 14 minutes. When done, the cookies should be firm to the touch. Turn the oven off, and leave the cookies in for 1 to 2 hours to harden.

Yield: Approximately 40 cookies

Carob Oat Cookies

$1/4$ cup honey
$1/2$ cup water
1 tsp pure vanilla extract
2 eggs
$1 1/2$ cups whole wheat flour
3 cups quick-cooking oats, uncooked
$1/3$ cup carob powderd
$1/2$ cup carob chips

In a large bowl, mix all the ingredients except the carob chips. Once well mixed, slowly stir in the carob chips. With a teaspoon, drop spoonfuls of dough on a baking sheet, about $1 1/2$ inches apart. Bake at 350 degrees for 10 to 15 minutes. When done, the cookies should be firm to the touch. Turn the oven off, and leave the cookies in for 1 to 2 hours to harden.

Yield: Approximately 90 cookies

Oatmeal and Raisin Cookies

Ingredients

1/4 cup vegetable oil
1/4 cup honey
1/2 cup skim milk
1 egg
1 Tbsp pure vanilla extract
1 1/2 cups quick-cooking
   oats, uncooked

1 1/2 cups whole wheat
   flour
1 tsp baking powder
1/2 cup all natural molasses
1/2 tsp baking soda
1/2 tsp ground cinnamon
1/2 tsp ground nutmeg

In a large bowl, mix all the ingredients. With a teaspoon, drop spoonfuls of dough onto a greased baking sheet, 1 inch apart. Bake at 375 degrees for 12 to 15 minutes. When done, the cookies should be firm to the touch. Turn the oven off, and leave the cookies in for 1 to 2 hours to harden.

Yield: Approximately 55 cookies

Carrot Oatmeal Cookies

Ingredients

¹⁄₂ cup unbleached white flour

¹⁄₂ cup whole wheat flour

1 ³⁄₄ cups quick-cooking oats, uncooked

¹⁄₄ cup low-fat powdered milk

¹⁄₄ tsp ground nutmeg

¹⁄₄ tsp ground cinnamon

¹⁄₄ cup vegetable oil

¹⁄₄ cup honey

¹⁄₂ cup all natural molasses

1 egg

1 cup carrots, shredded

1 tsp pure vanilla extract

¹⁄₃ cup water

In a large bowl, mix all the ingredients. With a teaspoon, drop spoonfuls of dough onto a greased baking sheet, 1 inch apart. Bake at 375 degrees for 10 to 12 minutes. When done, the cookies should be firm to the touch. Turn the oven off, and leave the cookies in for 1 to 2 hours to harden.

Yield: Approximately 45 cookies

Oatmeal Coconut Cookies

1 ½ cups whole wheat flour
1 cup quick-cooking oats, uncooked
½ cup unsweetened flaked coconut
½ cup carob chips

1 egg
1 tsp pure vanilla extract
¼ cup honey
½ cup vegetable oil
½ cup all natural applesauce, no sugar added

In a large bowl, mix all the ingredients. With a teaspoon, drop spoonfuls of dough onto a baking sheet, 1 inch apart. Bake at 375 degrees for 12 to 15 minutes. When done, the cookies should be firm to the touch. Turn the oven off, and leave the cookies in for 1 to 2 hours to harden.

Yield: Approximately 40 cookies
Available at health food stores and some grocery stores

Walnut Apple Cookies

⅓ cup unsalted walnuts, chopped

1 cup unbleached white flour

¼ cup honey

½ cup all natural apple-sauce, no sugar added

1 tsp pure vanilla extract

In a large bowl, mix all the ingredients. With a tea-spoon, drop spoonfuls of dough onto a greased baking sheet, 1 inch apart. Bake at 350 degrees for 12 to 15 minutes. When done, the cookies should be firm to the touch. Turn the oven off, and leave the cookies in for 1 to 2 hours to harden.

Yield: Approximately 20 cookies

Cakes

Cream Cheese Cake

$1/2$ cup all natural applesauce, no sugar added
2 eggs
$1/2$ cup water
4 oz cream cheese, softened
1 tsp pure vanilla extract

$1/4$ cup honey
2 cups unbleached white flour
2 tsp baking powder
$1/2$ tsp baking soda
$1/2$ cup wheat germ

In a medium bowl, mix all the wet ingredients. In a large bowl, mix all the dry ingredients. Slowly add the wet ingredients to the dry mixture. Mix the batter well. Pour into a greased 9- by 13-inch baking pan. Bake at 350 degrees for 40 to 45 minutes. The cake is completely cooked when a toothpick inserted in the center comes out clean. Cool in the pan.

Yield: 1 cake

Walnut Yogurt Cake

$1/2$ cup unsalted walnuts, chopped
$1/3$ cup honey
2 cups unbleached white flour
$1 1/2$ tsp baking powder

$1/2$ tsp baking soda
$1/2$ tsp ground cinnamon
1 cup all natural apple-sauce, no sugar added
2 eggs
1 cup low-fat plain yogurt

In a large bowl, mix all the ingredients. Pour the batter into a greased and floured 9- by 13- by 2-inch baking pan. Bake at 350 degrees for 30 to 35 minutes. The cake is completely cooked when a toothpick inserted in the center comes out clean. Cool the cake completely on a wire rack.

Yield: 1 cake

Carrot Cake

3 carrots, shredded
$\frac{1}{3}$ cup honey
$\frac{1}{4}$ cup vegetable oil
1 egg
1 cup whole wheat flour

$\frac{1}{3}$ cup wheat germ
1 tsp baking soda
1 tsp baking powder
$\frac{1}{2}$ tsp ground cinnamon
$\frac{1}{4}$ tsp ground ginger

In a medium bowl, mix all the wet ingredients. In a large bowl, mix all the dry ingredients. Slowly add the wet ingredients to the dry mixture. Mix the batter very well. Pour into a greased 9-inch round baking pan. Bake at 350 degrees for 25 to 35 minutes. The cake is completely cooked when a toothpick inserted in the center comes out clean. Cool in the pan.

Yield: 1 cake

Gingerbread Cake

$\frac{1}{4}$ cup all natural
  molasses
$\frac{1}{3}$ cup water
1 $\frac{1}{4}$ cups whole wheat
  flour
1 tsp baking soda

1 tsp baking powder
$\frac{1}{2}$ Tbsp ground ginger
1 tsp ground cinnamon
$\frac{1}{4}$ cup vegetable oil
$\frac{1}{4}$ cup honey
1 egg

In a large bowl, mix all the ingredients. Pour the batter into a greased and floured 8-inch round cake pan. Bake at 350 degrees for 25 to 35 minutes. The cake is completely cooked when a toothpick inserted in the center comes out clean. Cool completely on a wire rack.

Yield: 1 cake

Doggy Birthday Cake

Cake

½ cup cornmeal
½ cup unbleached white
    flour
1 cup whole wheat flour
1 tsp baking soda
1 tsp all natural molasses

¼ cup honey
1 egg
1 cup water
¼ cup freeze-dried liver ❧
1 tsp baking powder

Frosting

8 oz low-fat cream
    cheese, softened

2 Tbsp honey
⅓ cup vegetable oil

Decorative Frosting (optional)

4 oz low-fat cream cheese,
    softened

¼ cup vegetable oil
¼ cup carob powder ♥

Put the liver in a blender, and blend to a powder. In a large bowl, mix the other ingredients. Pour the batter into a greased and floured 8- by 8- by 2-inch baking pan. Bake at 350 degrees for 25 minutes. The cake is completely cooked when a toothpick inserted in the center comes out clean. Cool the cake completely on a wire rack. (Often, I cut the cake into the shape of a dog bone. Before frosting the cake, make a stencil in the shape of a dog bone. Place the stencil on the cake, and cut the cake to the shape. Then frost and decorate as desired.) To prepare the frosting, mix the cream cheese, honey, and oil until smooth. Spread a thin layer of frosting over the cooled cake. Mix the ingredients for the decorative frosting until smooth. Place the mixture in a piping bag, and decorate the cake.

Yield: 1 cake
❧ Available from pet stores
♥ Available at health food stores and some grocery stores

Pumpkin Cake Roll with Cream Cheese Filling

Ingredients

Cake

3 eggs

$1/4$ cup honey

$2/3$ cup solid-pack pumpkin

$3/4$ cup whole wheat flour

1 tsp baking powder

2 tsp ground cinnamon

$1/2$ tsp ground nutmeg

1 tsp ground ginger

$1/2$ cup all natural apple-
sauce, no sugar added

1 tsp baking soda

Filling

8 oz low-fat cream
cheese, softened

1 tsp pure vanilla extract

1 tsp honey

$1/4$ cup vegetable oil

In a large bowl, mix all the ingredients for the cake. Line a 9- by 13-inch jelly-roll pan with wax paper. Pour the batter into the pan, and spread it evenly. Bake at 375 degrees for 12 to 13 minutes. The cake is completely cooked when a toothpick inserted in the center comes out clean. Remove the cake immediately from the pan and place onto a towel. Remove the wax paper, and roll the cake and towel together. Cool completely. In a small bowl, mix the ingredients for the cream cheese filling. When the cake is cool, unroll and spread the cream cheese filling across the cake; reroll and serve. (Sometimes I have difficulty rolling the cake. If you do not want to roll the cake, you can cut the cake into equal portions. Add filling thinly between the slices, putting one slice on top of the other until all the slices are used. Frost the entire cake with the filling.)

Yield: 1 cake

Oatmeal Cake

Ingredients

Cake

1 cup quick-cooking oats, uncooked

¼ cup vegetable oil

¼ cup honey

1½ cups whole wheat flour

2 eggs

1 tsp ground cinnamon

½ tsp ground nutmeg

1 tsp pure vanilla extract

½ cup unsalted walnuts, chopped

Frosting

8 oz cream cheese, softened

⅓ cup vegetable oil

2 tsp orange rind, grated

In a large bowl, mix all the cake ingredients. Pour the batter into a greased and floured 8- by 16- by 2-inch baking pan. Bake at 350 degrees for 35 to 45 minutes. The cake is completely cooked when a toothpick inserted in the center comes out clean. Cool the cake completely on a wire rack. When the cake has cooled, make the frosting. Beat the cream cheese and vegetable oil until creamy. Gradually beat in the orange rind. Spread the frosting evenly over the cake.

Yield: 1 cake

Applesauce Spice Cake

Ingredients

Cake

2 ½ cups whole wheat flour
⅓ cup honey
1 ½ tsp baking soda
½ tsp baking powder
1 tsp ground cinnamon
½ tsp allspice
½ cup vegetable oil
2 eggs
2 cups all natural apple-sauce, no sugar added

Frosting

⅓ cup vegetable oil
8 oz cream cheese, softened
1 tsp pure vanilla extract

In a large bowl, mix all the cake ingredients. Pour the batter into a greased and floured 9- by 13- by 2-inch baking pan. Bake at 350 degrees for 45 to 50 minutes. The cake is completely cooked when a toothpick inserted in the center comes out clean. Cool the cake completely on a wire rack. When the cake has cooled, make the frosting. Beat the cream cheese, vegetable oil, and vanilla until creamy. Spread the frosting evenly over the cake.

Yield: 1 cake

Sour Cream Banana Cake

Cake

3 ½ cups whole wheat flour
1 tsp baking soda
¼ cup honey
½ cup vegetable oil
1 cup all natural apple-sauce, no sugar added

2 eggs
2 bananas, mashed
½ cup sour cream
2 tsp pure vanilla extract
¼ cup unsalted walnuts, chopped

Frosting

¼ cup sour cream
1 tsp pure vanilla extract

¼ cup honey
½ cup vegetable oil

In a large bowl, mix all the cake ingredients. Pour the batter into a greased and floured 9- by 13- by 2-inch baking pan. Bake at 350 degrees for 45 to 50 minutes. The cake is completely cooked when a toothpick inserted in the center comes out clean. Cool the cake completely on a wire rack. When the cake has cooled, make the frosting. Beat the sour cream, vegetable oil, honey, and vanilla until creamy. If the frosting is too soft, cover and refrigerate it until it thickens. Once thick, spread the frosting evenly over the cake.

Yield: 1 cake

Apple Raisin Cake

Ingredients

$\frac{1}{4}$ cup honey

$\frac{1}{2}$ cup vegetable oil

1 egg, beaten

2 apples, chopped, with skins and
  cores removed

$\frac{1}{2}$ cup raisins

1 $\frac{1}{2}$ cups whole wheat flour

1 tsp baking powder

$\frac{1}{2}$ tsp baking soda

$\frac{1}{2}$ tsp ground nutmeg

$\frac{1}{2}$ cup wheat germ

In a medium bowl, mix all the wet ingredients, including the apples and raisins. In a large bowl, mix all the dry ingredients. Slowly add the wet ingredients to the dry mixture. Mix the batter very well. Pour into a greased 9-inch square baking pan. Bake at 350 degrees for 40 to 45 minutes. The cake is completely cooked when a toothpick inserted in the center comes out clean. Cool in the pan.

Yield: 1 cake

Muffins

Apple Walnut Muffins

2 cups unbleached white
   flour
1 tsp ground cinnamon
2 eggs
$^1/_4$ cup honey
$^1/_2$ cup water
$^1/_4$ cup skim milk
$^1/_4$ cup vegetable oil

$^1/_2$ cup apple, diced, with
   skin and core removed
$^1/_2$ cup unsalted walnuts,
   chopped
$^1/_2$ cup wheat germ
1 tsp baking soda
1 tsp baking powder

In a bowl, mix all the ingredients until well blended. Spoon the batter into muffin cups, $^3/_4$ full. Bake at 375 degrees for 20 to 35 minutes. The bread is completely cooked when a toothpick inserted in the center comes out clean. Let them cool, and then remove them from the pan.

Yield: Approximately 12 muffins

Cornbread and Cheese Muffins

1 cup cornmeal
1 cup unbleached
   white flour

1 Tbsp honey
1 egg
1 cup cottage cheese

$^1/_2$ cup water
1 tsp baking powder
1 tsp baking soda

In a bowl, mix all the ingredients until blended. Spoon the batter into muffin cups, $^3/_4$ full. Bake at 400 degrees for 25 to 30 minutes. The muffins are completely baked when a toothpick inserted in the center comes out clean. Let them cool, and then remove them from the pan.

Yield: Approximately 12 muffins

Oatmeal Raisin Muffins

1 cup quick-cooking
  oats, uncooked
1 cup unbleached white
  flour
1/2 cup raisins
1/4 cup honey

1 cup water
1/3 cup vegetable oil
1 tsp pure vanilla extract
1 egg
1 tsp baking soda
1 tsp baking powder

In a large bowl, mix all the ingredients well. Spoon the batter into muffin cups, 3/4 full. Bake at 400 degrees for 18 to 20 minutes. The muffins are completely baked when a toothpick inserted in the center comes out clean. Let them cool, and then remove them from the pan.

Yield: Approximately 12 muffins

Cream Cheese Muffins

4 oz cream cheese,
  softened
1/4 cup honey
1 tsp pure vanilla extract
1 egg
3/4 cup water

1/4 cup vegetable oil
2 cups unbleached white
  flour
1 tsp baking soda
1 tsp baking powder

In a bowl, mix all the ingredients until blended. Spoon the batter into muffin cups, 3/4 full. Bake at 375 degrees for 25 to 30 minutes. The muffins are completely baked when a toothpick inserted in the center comes out clean. Let them cool, and then remove them from the pan.

Yield: Approximately 12 muffins

Carob Nut Muffins

Ingredients

2 ½ cups whole wheat flour
½ cup unsalted walnuts, chopped
½ cup carob chips
¼ cup honey
⅓ cup vegetable oil
½ cup skim milk

½ cup water
1 tsp pure vanilla extract
1 egg
1 tsp baking powder
1 tsp baking soda

In a large bowl, mix all the ingredients well. Spoon the batter into muffin cups, ¾ full. Bake at 400 degrees for 18 to 20 minutes. The bread is completely cooked when a toothpick inserted in the center comes out clean. Let them cool, and then remove them from the pan.

Yield: Approximately 12 muffins
Available at health food stores and some grocery stores

Corn Muffins

1 cup cornmeal
1 cup unbleached white
  flour
¼ cup honey
½ cup skim milk

½ cup water
¼ cup vegetable oil
1 egg
1 tsp baking soda
1 tsp baking powder

In a large bowl, mix all the ingredients well. Spoon the batter into muffin cups, ¾ full. Bake at 400 degrees for 18 to 20 minutes. The muffins are completely baked when a toothpick inserted in the center comes out clean. Let them cool, and then remove them from the pan.

Yield: Approximately 12 muffins

Zucchini Basil Muffins

1 ¾ cups whole wheat
  flour
3 Tbsp Parmesan cheese,
  grated
1 Tbsp honey

2 tsp baking powder
1 egg
¾ cup skim milk
¼ cup vegetable oil
½ cup zucchini, shredded

1 Tbsp of finely chopped
  fresh basil or ½ tsp
  dried basil
1 tsp baking soda

In a large bowl, mix all the ingredients until blended; then beat the batter for 2 minutes. Spoon the batter into muffin cups, ¾ full. Bake at 400 degrees for 22 to 24 minutes. The muffins are completely baked when a toothpick inserted in the center comes out clean. Let them cool, and then remove them from the pan.

Yield: Approximately 12 muffins

Zucchini Muffins

Ingredients

1 cup whole wheat flour
½ tsp ground nutmeg
2 eggs
¼ cup honey
¼ cup all natural apple-
   sauce, no sugar added

1 ½ cups zucchini,
   shredded
½ cup unsalted walnuts,
   chopped
1 tsp baking soda
1 tsp baking powder

In a large bowl, mix all the ingredients well. Spoon the batter into muffin cups, ¾ full. Bake at 375 degrees for 20 to 25 minutes. The muffins are completely baked when a toothpick inserted in the center comes out clean. Let them cool, and then remove them from the pan.

Yield: Approximately 12 muffins

Banana Wheat Germ Muffins

2 cups unbleached white
   flour
$1/2$ cup banana, mashed
2 Tbsp wheat germ
1 tsp pure vanilla extract
$1/4$ cup honey

1 cup water
$1/3$ cup vegetable oil
1 egg
1 tsp baking soda
1 tsp baking powder

In a large bowl, mix all the ingredients well. Spoon the batter into muffin cups, $3/4$ full. Bake at 400 degrees for 20 to 25 minutes. The muffins are completely baked when a toothpick inserted in the center and comes out clean. Let them cool, and then remove them from the pan.

Yield: Approximately 12 muffins

Zucchini Carob Muffins

2 cups whole wheat flour
$1/4$ cup honey
3 Tbsp carob powderd
2 eggs
$1/4$ cup vegetable oil

$1/2$ cup all natural apple-
   sauce, no sugar added
1 tsp pure vanilla extract
1 cup zucchini, shredded
$1/2$ cup carob chips☙

$1/4$ cup unsalted peanuts,
   chopped
1 tsp baking soda
1 tsp baking powder

In a bowl, mix all the ingredients until blended. Spoon the batter into muffin cups, $3/4$ full. Bake at 375 degrees for 20 to 25 minutes. The muffins are completely baked when a toothpick inserted in the center comes out clean. Let them cool, and then remove them from the pan.

Yield: Approximately 12 muffins
☙Available at health food stores and some grocery stores

Healthy Muffins

Ingredients

1 pear, grated, skin and core removed

3 carrots, grated

1/4 cup honey

2 3/4 cups water

1/4 tsp pure vanilla extract

1 egg

4 cups whole wheat flour

1/4 cup white raisins

1 Tbsp baking powder

2 Tbsp ground cinnamon

1 Tbsp ground nutmeg

1 tsp baking soda

1/2 cup wheat germ

In a large bowl, mix all the ingredients except the wheat germ; then beat the batter for 1 minute. Spoon the batter into muffin cups, 3/4 full. Sprinkle the top of each muffin with wheat germ. Bake at 400 degrees for 25 to 30 minutes. The muffins are completely baked when a toothpick inserted in the center comes out clean. Let them cool, and then remove them from the pan.

Yield: Approximately 12 muffins

Carrot and Yogurt Muffins

Muffins

4 carrots, grated

1 1/4 cups whole wheat flour

1/2 cup unbleached white flour

1/4 cup wheat germ

1 tsp baking soda

1 tsp baking powder

1 tsp ground cinnamon

2 eggs

8 oz natural low-fat plain yogurt

1/4 cup honey

3 Tbsp vegetable oil

1/4 cup raisins

Frosting

4 oz low-fat cream cheese, softened

2 tsp pure vanilla extract

1/4 cup vegetable oil

In a large bowl, mix all the ingredients for the muffins; then beat the batter for 1 minute. Spoon the batter into muffin cups, 3/4 full. Bake at 350 degrees for 20 to 25 minutes. The muffins are completely baked when a toothpick inserted in the center comes out clean. Cool the muffins completely on a wire rack. Mix the frosting ingredients until smooth, and frost the cooled muffins. Optional: Decorate the tops of the uncooked muffins with carob powder, chopped peanuts (no salt added), wheat germ, or carob chips. Let them cool, and then remove them from the pan.

Yield: Approximately 12 muffins

Peanut Butter Muffins

1 ¾ cups whole wheat flour
1 cup skim milk
¼ cup honey
½ cup all natural peanut but-
    ter, no salt or sugar added

¼ cup vegetable oil
1 tsp baking powder
1 tsp pure vanilla extract
2 eggs
1 tsp baking soda

In a bowl, mix all the ingredients until blended; then beat the batter for 2 minutes. Spoon the batter into muffin cups, ¾ full. Bake at 350 degrees for 18 to 20 minutes. The muffins are completely baked when a toothpick inserted in the center comes out clean. Let them cool, and then remove them from the pan.

Yield: Approximately 12 muffins

Sour Cream Carob Chip Muffins

2 Tbsp vegetable oil
⅓ cup honey
1 tsp pure vanilla extract
½ cup sour cream
1 egg

¾ tsp baking soda
¾ tsp baking powder
1 ½ cups whole wheat flour
½ cup carob
    chips

In a bowl, mix all the ingredients until blended. Spoon the batter into muffin cups, ¾ full. Bake at 350 degrees for 18 to 20 minutes. The muffins are completely baked when a toothpick inserted in the center comes out clean. Let them cool, and then remove them from the pan.

Yield: Approximately 12 muffins
Available at health food stores and some grocery stores

Carob Chip and Corn Muffins

½ cup carob chips🐾
¾ cup whole wheat flour
1 cup cornmeal
1 Tbsp honey
2 tsp baking powder

1 cup water
2 eggs
¼ cup vegetable oil
1 tsp baking soda

In a large bowl, mix all the ingredients until blended; then beat the batter for 1 minute. Spoon the batter into muffin cups, ¾ full. Bake at 400 degrees for 15 to 18 minutes. The muffins are completely baked when a toothpick inserted in the center comes out clean. Let them cool, and then remove them from the pan.

Yield: Approximately 12 muffins

Banana Carob Chip Muffins

1 ¾ cups whole wheat flour
¼ cup honey
½ cup carob chips🐾
1 egg
¼ cup vegetable oil

¼ cup milk
1 banana, mashed
1 tsp baking powder
1 tsp baking soda

In a bowl, mix all the ingredients until blended. Spoon the batter into muffin cups, ¾ full. Bake at 400 degrees for 20 to 25 minutes. The muffins are completely baked when a toothpick inserted in the center comes out clean. Let them cool, and then remove them from the pan.

Yield: Approximately 12 muffins
🐾Available at health food stores and some grocery stores

Cheddar Apple Bran Muffins

½ cup whole bran cereal
¼ cup water
1 apple, chopped, with
   skin and core removed
⅓ cup vegetable oil
1 egg
1 ½ cups unbleached
   white flour

1 tsp ground cinnamon
⅓ cup honey
¼ cup low-fat cheddar
   cheese, shredded
1 tsp baking soda
1 tsp baking powder

In a bowl, mix all the ingredients until blended. Spoon the batter into muffin cups, ¾ full. Bake at 375 degrees for 20 to 25 minutes. The muffins are completely baked when a toothpick inserted in the center comes out clean. Let them cool, and then remove them from the pan.

Yield: Approximately 12 muffins

Carrot Muffins

Ingredients

2 cups unbleached white
  flour

2 tsp baking soda

2 tsp ground cinnamon

¼ cup honey

2 carrots, shredded

½ cup raisins

½ cup unsalted walnuts,
  chopped

2 eggs

1 cup all natural apple-
  sauce, no sugar added

2 tsp pure vanilla extract

1 tsp baking soda

1 tsp baking powder

In a bowl, mix all the ingredients until blended. Spoon the batter into muffin cups, ¾ full. Bake at 350 degrees for 15 to 20 minutes. The muffins are completely baked when a toothpick inserted in the center comes out clean. Let them cool, and then remove them from the pan.

Yield: Approximately 18 muffins

Pumpkin Muffins

2 ½ cups unbleached white flour
¼ cup vegetable oil
1 tsp pure vanilla extract
½ cup unsalted peanuts, chopped

1 tsp baking soda
1 tsp baking powder
½ cup all natural applesauce, no
    sugar added

1 egg
1 cup solid-pack pumpkin
¼ cup honey

In a bowl, mix all the ingredients until blended. Spoon the batter into muffin cups, ¾ full. Bake at 375 degrees for 25 to 30 minutes. The muffins are completely baked when a toothpick inserted in the center comes out clean. Let them cool, and then remove them from the pan.

Yield: Approximately 8 muffins

Cinnamon Walnut Muffins

2 cups whole wheat flour
¼ cup unsalted walnuts,
    chopped
¼ cup honey
½ tsp ground cinnamon

1 egg
¼ cup water
¼ cup vegetable oil
1 tsp baking soda
1 tsp baking powder

In a bowl, mix all the ingredients until blended. Spoon the batter into muffin cups, ¾ full. Bake at 400 degrees for 20 to 25 minutes. The muffins are completely baked when a toothpick inserted in the center comes out clean. Let them cool, and then remove them from the pan.

Yield: Approximately 12 muffins

Frozen Treats

Banana Split

Ingredients

4 bananas, cut into small chunks

½ cup carob powderd

¼ cup unsalted peanuts, chopped

1 cup natural low-fat plain yogurt

¼ cup honey

Mix all the ingredients in a blender, and blend well; the mixture should be fairly thick. Pour the mixture into ice cube trays, cover with plastic wrap, and freeze. When the cubes are frozen, place them in a zipper-locking plastic storage bag. Crush the cubes with a rolling pin, and allow them to soften. Serve the crushed cubes, and freeze the remaining crushed cubes in the plastic storage bag. (I often sprinkle granola pieces over the crushed cubes.)

Yield: Approximately 1 ½ cups

🐾Available at health food stores and some grocery stores

Strawberry Frost

2 ³/₄ cups frozen
    strawberries
1 cup low-fat vanilla yogurt

¹/₄ cup honey
¹/₂ tsp pure vanilla
    extract

Place all the ingredients in a blender or food processor, cover, and blend until smooth. If you are not going to serve the strawberry frost immediately, pour the mixture into a freezer-safe container. Freeze until firm. Remove the container from the freezer, and allow the frost to soften before serving.

Yield: Approximately 2 ¹/₃ cups

Banana Cream Ice

2 cups low-fat sour cream
¹/₄ cup water

4 bananas, chopped
¹/₄ cup honey

Place all the ingredients in a blender or food processor, cover, and blend until smooth. Pour the mixture into a freezer-safe container. Freeze until firm. Remove the container from the freezer, and allow the ice cream to soften before serving.

Yield: Approximately 3 cups

Frozen Strawberry Bars

Ingredients

1 cup unbleached white flour
¼ cup unsalted peanuts, chopped
½ cup vegetable oil
2 egg whites
¼ cup honey

10 oz frozen strawberries, partially thawed
2 Tbsp lemon juice
1 cup low-fat vanilla yogurt
½ cup wheat germ

Combine the flour, peanuts, and vegetable oil in a bowl, mixing well. Spread the mixture in 9- by 13- by 2-inch baking pan. Bake at 350 degrees for 20 to 25 minutes. While the crust is baking, combine the egg whites, honey, strawberries, and lemon juice in a large mixing bowl. Beat with an electric mixer at high speed for 15 minutes. Fold in the vanilla yogurt. Pour the strawberry mixture into the baked crust; top the mixture with wheat germ, and freeze until firm. Remove the baking pan from the freezer, and allow the mixture to soften before cutting into 2-inch squares and serving.

Yield: Approximately 16 bars

Fruity Cooler

1 cup water
½ cup cantaloupe, cubed,
    with seeds and rind
    removed

½ cup pineapple chunks in
    their own juices, drained
1 banana, sliced
2 Tbsp honey

Place all the ingredients in a blender or food processor, cover, and blend until smooth. Pour the mixture into a freezer-safe container, and freeze until firm. Remove the container from the freezer, and allow the cooler to soften before serving.

Yield: Approximately 3 cups

Fruit Dog Sherbet

¼ cup apple, chopped,
    with skin and core
    removed
¼ cup seedless grapes,
    chopped, with skins
    removed

¼ cup peach, chopped,
    with skin and pit
    removed
1 cup natural low-fat
    vanilla yogurt
2 Tbsp honey

Mix all the ingredients in a blender. Blend until smooth. Pour the mixture into ice cube trays, cover with plastic wrap, and freeze. When the cubes are frozen, place them in a zipper-locking plastic storage bag. Crush the cubes with a rolling pin, and allow them to soften. Serve the crushed cubes, and freeze the remaining crushed cubes in the plastic storage bag. (I often sprinkle granola pieces over the crushed cubes.)

Yield: Approximately 1 ½ cups

Peach Dog Sherbet

²/₃ cup water

¹/₃ cup honey

4 cups fresh peaches, with pits and skins removed

Place all ingredients in a blender or food processor, cover, and blend until smooth. Pour the mixture into a freezer-safe container, and freeze until firm. Remove the container from the freezer, and allow the sherbet to soften before serving.

Yield: Approximately 5 cups

Fancy Strawberry Dog Sherbet

10 oz package frozen strawberries, partially thawed

³/₄ cup water

¹/₂ cup skim milk

¹/₄ cup honey

2 egg whites

Place the strawberry, water, milk, and honey in a blender; cover; and blend until smooth. In a medium bowl, beat the egg whites with an electric mixer on medium speed until soft peaks form. Then continue beating on high speed until stiff peaks form. Fold the egg white mixture into the strawberry mixture. Pour the mixture into a 9- by 9- by 2-inch pan. Cover and freeze until firm. To serve, scrape a spoon across the frozen mixture, and put the shavings in your dog's bowl.

Yield: Approximately 16 servings

Tropical Fruit Dog Sherbet

10 oz frozen strawberries,
thawed
½ cup crushed pineapple in
its own juices, drained

⅓ cup low-fat vanilla yogurt
1 ripe banana, mashed

Place all ingredients in a blender or food processor, cover, and blend until smooth. Pour the mixture into a freezer-safe container, and freeze until firm. Remove the container from the freezer, and allow the sherbet to soften before serving.

Yield: Approximately 2 cups

Raspberry Dog Sherbet

2 cups low-fat plain
yogurt
¼ cup honey

12 oz frozen raspberries
¼ cup water

Place all the ingredients in a blender or food processor, cover, and blend until smooth. Pour the mixture into a freezer-safe container, and freeze until firm. Remove the container from the freezer, and allow the sherbet to soften before serving.

Yield: Approximately 4 cups

Cantaloupe Dog Sherbet

1 ½ cups cantaloupe, cubed,
    with seeds and rind
    removed

3 cups water
⅓ cup honey
2 tsp pure vanilla extract

Place all the ingredients in a blender or food processor, cover, and blend until smooth. Pour the mixture into a freezer-safe container, and freeze until firm. Remove the container from the freezer, and allow the sherbet to soften before serving.

Yield: Approximately 5 cups

Lemon Mint Dog Sherbet

¼ cup honey
2 Tbsp fresh mint leaves,
    chopped

2 ½ cups water
¼ cup real lemon juice

Place all the ingredients in a blender or food processor, cover, and blend until smooth. Pour the mixture into a freezer-safe container, and freeze until firm. Remove the container from the freezer, and allow the sherbet to soften before serving.

Yield: Approximately 2 ½ cups

Watermelon Dog Sherbet

Ingredients

2 cups watermelon
chunks, with seeds
and rind removed

3 cups water
1 Tbsp real lemon
juice

Place all the ingredients in a blender or food processor, cover, and blend until smooth. Pour the mixture into a freezer-safe container, and freeze until firm. Remove the container from the freezer, and allow the sherbet to soften before serving.

Yield: Approximately 5 cups

Blueberry Cream

1 cup water
1 cup nonfat plain yogurt
½ cup sour cream
¼ cup honey
½ cup fresh blueberries

Place all the ingredients in a blender or food processor, cover, and blend until smooth. Pour the mixture into a freezer-safe container, and freeze until firm. Remove the container from the freezer, and allow the cream to soften before serving.

Yield: Approximately 3 cups

Peaches and Cream

2 cups vanilla yogurt
½ cup sour cream
¼ cup honey
2 cups of peaches in their own juices, drained and chopped

Place all the ingredients in a blender or food processor, cover, and blend until smooth. Pour the mixture into a freezer-safe container, and freeze until firm. Remove the container from the freezer, and allow the cream to soften before serving.

Yield: Approximately 5 cups

Strawberry Banana Yogurt

2 cups vanilla yogurt
½ cup frozen strawberries
1 banana, chopped

⅓ cup water
¼ cup honey
½ cup carob chips❀

Place all the ingredients in a blender or food processor, cover, and blend until smooth. Pour the mixture into a freezer-safe container, and freeze until firm. Remove the container from the freezer, and allow the yogurt to soften before serving.

Yield: Approximately 3 cups
❀Available at health food stores and some grocery stores

Carob Nut Frozen Yogurt

¼ cup honey
1 egg
6 Tbsp carob powderd
2 cups plain yogurt

1 cup water
¼ cup unsalted walnuts,
   chopped

Place all the ingredients in a blender or food processor, cover, and blend until smooth. Pour the mixture into a freezer-safe container, and freeze until firm. Remove the container from the freezer, and allow the yogurt to soften before serving.

Yield: Approximately 3 ½ cups

Index